Contents

Cornbread Chicken Pot Pie

PREP: 10 minutes • **BAKE:** 40 minutes

- **1 can (10¾ ounces) Campbell's® Condensed Cream of Chicken Soup (Regular or 98% Fat Free)**
- **½ cup milk**
- **⅛ teaspoon ground black pepper**
- **1 can (about 8 ounces) whole kernel corn, drained**
- **2 cups cubed cooked chicken**
- **1 package (11 ounces) refrigerated cornbread twists or breadsticks**

1. Stir the soup, milk, black pepper, corn and chicken in a 2-quart casserole.
2. Bake at 425°F. for 20 minutes.
3. Separate the cornbread into **8** pieces along perforations. (Do not unroll dough.) Place over the hot chicken mixture.
4. Bake for 20 minutes more or until the bread is golden.

***Makes:* 4 servings**

Baked Macaroni & Cheese

PREP: 20 minutes • **BAKE:** 20 minutes

- **1 can (10¾ ounces) Campbell's® Condensed Cheddar Cheese Soup**
- **½ soup can milk**
- **⅛ teaspoon ground black pepper**
- **1½ cups corkscrew-shaped (rotini) or medium shell pasta, cooked and drained**
- **1 tablespoon dry bread crumbs**
- **2 teaspoons butter, melted**

1. Stir the soup, milk, black pepper and pasta in a 1-quart casserole.
2. Mix the bread crumbs with the butter in a small bowl. Sprinkle over the pasta mixture.
3. Bake at 400°F. for 20 minutes or until hot.

Makes: 4 servings

Baked Pork Chops with Garden Stuffing

PREP: 10 minutes • **BAKE:** 40 minutes

Vegetable cooking spray

1 can (10¾ ounces) Campbell's® Condensed Golden Mushroom Soup

¾ cup water

1 bag (16 ounces) frozen vegetable combination (broccoli, cauliflower, carrots)

1 tablespoon butter

4 cups Pepperidge Farm® Herb Seasoned Stuffing

6 boneless pork chops, ¾ inch thick

1. Spray a 13×9×2-inch (3-quart) shallow baking dish with cooking spray.

2. Stir ⅓ **cup** of the soup, ½ **cup** of the water, vegetables and butter in a 2-quart saucepan over medium-high heat to a boil. Remove from the heat. Add the stuffing and stir lightly to coat.

3. Spoon the stuffing mixture into the prepared dish. Arrange the chops over the stuffing mixture.

4. Stir the remaining soup and remaining water in a small bowl. Spoon the soup mixture over the chops.

5. Bake at 400°F. for 40 minutes or until the chops are cooked through.

Makes: 6 servings

Chicken Scampi and Rice Bake

PREP: 10 minutes • **BAKE:** 40 minutes

- 1 can ($10\frac{3}{4}$ ounces) Campbell's® Condensed Cream of Chicken Soup (Regular **or** 98% Fat Free)
- $1\frac{1}{3}$ cups water
- 2 tablespoons lemon juice
- 3 cloves garlic, minced **or** $\frac{3}{4}$ teaspoon garlic powder
- $\frac{3}{4}$ cup **uncooked** regular long-grain white rice
- 4 skinless, boneless chicken breast halves
- 2 slices lemon, cut in half

1. Stir the soup, water, lemon juice, garlic and rice in an 11×8-inch (2-quart) shallow baking dish. Top with the chicken. **Cover.**

2. Bake at 400°F. for 40 minutes or until the chicken is cooked through. Stir the mixture before serving. Garnish with lemon.

Makes: 4 servings

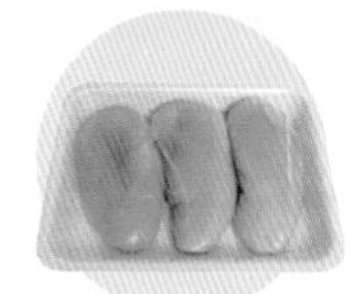

Chicken Mozzarella

PREP: 5 minutes • **BAKE:** 20 minutes

4 skinless, boneless chicken breast halves

1 can (10¾ ounces) Campbell's® Condensed Tomato Soup (Regular or Healthy Request®)

½ teaspoon Italian seasoning or dried oregano leaves, crushed

½ teaspoon garlic powder

¼ cup shredded mozzarella cheese

3 cups corkscrew-shaped pasta (rotini), cooked without salt and drained

1. Place the chicken in an 11×8-inch (2-quart) shallow baking dish. Stir the soup, Italian seasoning and garlic powder in a small bowl. Spoon the soup mixture over the chicken.

2. Bake at 400°F. for 20 minutes or until the chicken is cooked through.

3. Sprinkle the cheese over the chicken. Serve with the pasta.

Makes: 4 servings

One-Dish Chicken & Rice Bake

PREP: 5 minutes • **BAKE:** 45 minutes

- **1 can (10¾ ounces) Campbell's® Condensed Cream of Mushroom Soup (Regular or 98% Fat Free)**
- **1⅓ cups water**
- **¾ cup uncooked regular long-grain white rice**
- **¼ teaspoon paprika**
- **¼ teaspoon ground black pepper**
- **4 skinless, boneless chicken breast halves**

1. Stir the soup, water, rice, paprika and black pepper in an 11×8-inch (2-quart) shallow baking dish. Top with the chicken. Sprinkle the chicken with additional paprika and black pepper. **Cover**.

2. Bake at 375°F. for 45 minutes or until the chicken is cooked through and the rice is tender.

Makes: 4 servings

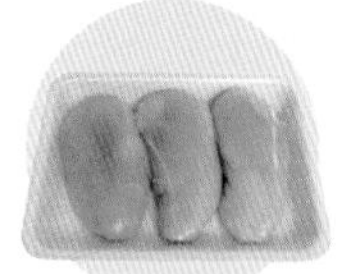

Chicken Enchilada-Style Casserole

PREP: 10 minutes • **BAKE:** 35 minutes

2 cans (10¾ ounces each) Campbell's® Condensed Cheddar Cheese Soup
½ cup water
1 jar (16 ounces) chunky salsa
4 cups cubed cooked chicken
8 (8-inch) flour or 12 (6-inch) corn tortillas, cut into strips
1 cup shredded Cheddar cheese (4 ounces)

1. Stir the soup, water, **½ cup** of the salsa and chicken in a large bowl. Stir in the tortillas. Spread the chicken mixture in a 13×9×2-inch (3-quart) shallow baking dish. Top with the cheese. **Cover**.

2. Bake at 350°F. for 35 minutes or until hot and bubbly. Serve with the remaining salsa.

Makes: 8 servings

Herb Roasted Chicken & Vegetables

PREP: 10 minutes • **BAKE:** 50 minutes

- **1 can (10¾ ounces) Campbell's® Condensed Cream of Mushroom Soup (Regular or 98% Fat Free)**
- **⅓ cup water**
- **2 teaspoons dried oregano leaves, crushed**
- **4 medium potatoes, cut into quarters**
- **2 cups fresh or frozen baby carrots**
- **4 skinless, boneless chicken breast halves**
- **½ teaspoon paprika**

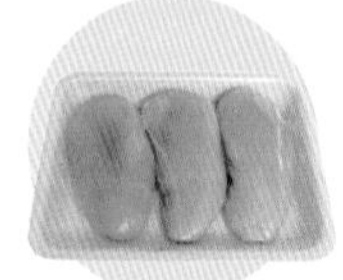

1. Stir the soup, water, **1 teaspoon** of the oregano, potatoes and carrots in a 17×11-inch shallow roasting pan. Top with the chicken. Sprinkle with the remaining oregano and paprika.

2. Bake at 400°F. for 50 minutes or until the chicken is cooked through. Stir the vegetables before serving.

Makes: 4 servings

Pennsylvania Dutch Ham & Noodle Casserole

PREP: 10 minutes • **BAKE:** 30 minutes

- **2 cans (10¾ ounces each) Campbell's® Condensed Cream of Mushroom Soup (Regular or 98% Fat Free)**
- **½ cup milk**
- **1 large onion, chopped (about 1 cup)**
- **4 cups cubed cooked ham (about 2 pounds)**
- **1 bag (16 ounces) extra-wide egg noodles, cooked and drained**
- **8 ounces extra-sharp Cheddar cheese, cut into pieces (2 cups)**

1. Stir the soup, milk, onion, ham, noodles and **1 cup** of the cheese in a 13×9×2-inch (3-quart) shallow baking dish. Top with the remaining cheese. **Cover**.
2. Bake at 400°F. for 30 minutes or until hot.

Makes: 4 servings

Easy Substitution: *Substitute cooked chicken **or** turkey for the ham.*

Sloppy Joe Casserole

PREP: 10 minutes • **BAKE:** 15 minutes

- **1 pound ground beef**
- **1 can (10¾ ounces) Campbell's® Condensed Tomato Soup (Regular or Healthy Request®)**
- **¼ cup water**
- **1 teaspoon Worcestershire sauce**
- **⅛ teaspoon ground black pepper**
- **1 package (7.5 ounces) refrigerated biscuits (10)**
- **½ cup shredded Cheddar cheese**

1. Cook the beef in a 10-inch skillet over medium-high heat until the beef is well browned, stirring frequently to break up meat. Pour off any fat.
2. Stir the soup, water, Worcestershire and black pepper into the skillet. Heat to a boil. Spoon the beef mixture into a 1½-quart casserole. Arrange the biscuits over beef mixture around edge of casserole.
3. Bake at 400°F. for 15 minutes or until the biscuits are golden brown. Sprinkle the cheese over beef mixture.

Makes: 5 servings

Beef Taco Bake

PREP: 10 minutes • **BAKE:** 30 minutes

- 1 pound ground beef
- 1 can (10¾ ounces) Campbell's® Condensed Tomato Soup (Regular **or** Healthy Request®)

- 1 cup chunky salsa **or** picante sauce

- ½ cup milk

- 6 (8-inch) flour tortillas **or** 8 (6-inch) corn tortillas, cut into 1-inch pieces

- 1 cup shredded Cheddar cheese (4 ounces)

1. Cook the beef in a 10-inch skillet over medium-high heat until the beef is well browned, stirring frequently to break up meat. Pour off any fat.
2. Stir the soup, salsa, milk, tortillas and ½ **cup** of the cheese into the skillet. Spoon soup mixture into an 11×8-inch (2-quart) shallow baking dish. **Cover**.
3. Bake at 400°F. for 30 minutes or until hot. Sprinkle with the remaining cheese.

Makes: 4 servings

Quick Chicken Noodle Bake

PREP: 10 minutes • **BAKE:** 30 minutes

- **1 can (10¾ ounces) Campbell's® Condensed Cream of Mushroom Soup (Regular or 98% Fat Free)**
- **½ cup milk**
- **1 cup cooked peas**
- **2 cups cubed cooked chicken**
- **2 cups medium egg noodles, cooked and drained**
- **⅓ cup dry bread crumbs**

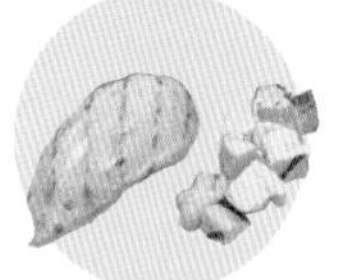

1. Stir the soup, milk, peas, chicken and noodles in a 1½-quart casserole.
2. Bake at 400°F. for 15 minutes. Stir.
3. Top with bread crumbs. Bake for 15 minutes more or until hot.

Makes: 4 servings

Chicken with White Beans

PREP: 10 minutes • **BAKE:** 50 minutes

- 2 cans (10¾ ounces **each**) Campbell's® Condensed Tomato Soup (Regular **or** Healthy Request®)
- 1 teaspoon dried oregano leaves, crushed
- ¼ teaspoon garlic powder **or** 2 cloves garlic, minced
- 2 cans (about 16 ounces **each**) white kidney (cannellini) beans, rinsed and drained
- 1 large onion, chopped (about 1 cup)
- 4 skinless, boneless chicken breast halves

1. Stir the soup, oregano, garlic powder, beans and onion in an 11×8-inch (2-quart) shallow baking dish.

2. Bake at 400°F. for 50 minutes or until the chicken is cooked through. Stir the mixture before serving.

Makes: 4 servings

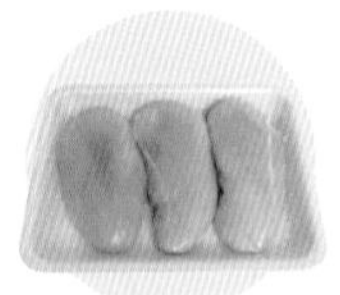

Turkey and Stuffing Casserole

PREP: 5 minutes • **BAKE:** 25 minutes

- **Vegetable cooking spray**
- **1 can (10¾ ounces) Campbell's® Condensed Cream of Mushroom Soup (Regular or 98% Fat Free)**
- **1 cup milk or water**
- **1 bag (16 ounces) frozen vegetable combination (broccoli, cauliflower, carrots), thawed**
- **2 cups cubed cooked turkey or chicken**
- **4 cups Pepperidge Farm® Cubed Herb Seasoned Stuffing**
- **1 cup shredded Swiss or Cheddar cheese (4 ounces)**

1. Spray an 11×8-inch (2-quart) shallow baking dish with cooking spray and set aside.
2. Stir the soup and milk in a large bowl. Stir in the vegetables, turkey and stuffing. Spoon the mixture into the prepared dish.
3. Bake at 400°F. for 20 minutes or until hot and bubbly. Stir.
4. Sprinkle the cheese over the turkey mixture. Bake for 5 minutes more or until the cheese melts.

***Makes:* 6 servings**

Easy Substitution Tip: *Substitute 1 can (9.75 ounces) Swanson® Premium White Chunk Chicken Breast, drained for the cubed cooked turkey.*

Tuna Rice Casserole

PREP: 10 minutes • **BAKE:** 50 minutes

- 1 can (10¾ ounces) Campbell's® Condensed Cream of Mushroom Soup (Regular **or** 98% Fat Free)
- 1½ cups milk
- 2 cans (about 6 ounces **each**) tuna, drained
- 4 ounces sliced American cheese, cut up (about 1 cup)
- ¾ cup **uncooked** regular long-grain white rice
- 2 tablespoons dry Italian-seasoned bread crumbs

1. Stir the soup, milk, tuna, cheese and rice in a 9-inch square baking dish. **Cover**.
2. Bake at 350°F. for 30 minutes. Stir.
3. Sprinkle the bread crumbs over the tuna mixture. Bake for 20 minutes more or until hot and bubbly and the rice is tender.

Makes: 4 servings

Broccoli & Noodles Supreme

PREP: 15 minutes • **BAKE:** 30 minutes

- 1 can (10¾ ounces) Campbell's® Condensed Cream of Chicken Soup (Regular **or** 98% Fat Free)
- 1 cup milk
- ⅛ teaspoon ground black pepper
- ½ cup sour cream
- ⅓ cup grated Parmesan cheese
- 2 cups fresh **or** frozen broccoli flowerets
- 2 cups **uncooked** medium egg noodles

1. Stir the soup, milk, black pepper, sour cream, cheese, broccoli and noodles into a 2-quart casserole. **Cover**.

2. Bake at 400°F. for 15 minutes. Stir.

3. Bake for 15 minutes more or until hot and bubbly.

***Makes:** 6 servings*

Chicken Broccoli Divan

PREP: 15 minutes • **BAKE:** 25 minutes

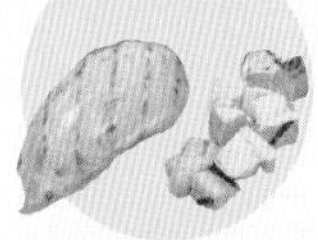

- **1 pound fresh broccoli, cut into spears or 1 package (about 10 ounces) frozen broccoli spears, cooked and drained**
- **1½ cups cubed cooked chicken or turkey**
- **1 can (10¾ ounces) Campbell's® Condensed Broccoli Cheese Soup (Regular or 98% Fat Free)**
- **⅓ cup milk**
- **½ cup shredded Cheddar cheese (optional)**

1. Arrange the broccoli and chicken in an 11×8-inch (2-quart) shallow baking dish.
2. Stir the soup and milk in a small bowl and pour over the broccoli and chicken mixture. Sprinkle the cheese over the soup mixture.
3. Bake at 400°F. for 25 minutes or until hot and bubbly.

***Makes:* 4 servings**

Easy Substitution: *Substitute 1 can (10¾ ounces) Campbell's® Condensed Cream of Chicken Soup (Regular* ***or*** *98% Fat Free) for the Broccoli Cheese Soup.*

Garlic Mashed Potatoes & Beef Bake

PREP: 10 minutes • **BAKE:** 20 minutes

- 1 pound ground beef **or** ground turkey
- 1 can (10¾ ounces) Campbell's® Condensed Cream of Mushroom with Roasted Garlic Soup
- 1 tablespoon Worcestershire sauce
- 1 bag (16 ounces) frozen vegetable combination (broccoli, cauliflower, carrots), thawed
- 2 cups water
- ¾ cup milk
- 2 cups instant mashed potato flakes **or** buds

1. Cook the beef in a 10-inch skillet over medium-high heat until the beef is well browned, stirring frequently to break up meat. Pour off any fat.

2. Stir the beef, ½ **can** of the soup, Worcestershire and vegetables in an 11×8-inch (2-quart) shallow baking dish.

3. Heat the water and remaining soup in a 2-quart saucepan over high heat to a boil. Stir in the milk. Slowly stir in the potatoes. Spoon the potatoes over the beef mixture.

4. Bake at 400°F. for 20 minutes or until hot.

***Makes:* 4 servings**

Time-Saving Tip: *To thaw vegetables, microwave on HIGH for 3 minutes.*

Italian Sub Casserole

PREP: 10 minutes • **BAKE:** 35 minutes

- **1½ pounds ground beef**
- **1 can (10¾ ounces) Campbell's® Condensed Tomato Soup (Regular or Healthy Request®)**
- **1 cup water**
- **½ teaspoon dried Italian seasoning**
- **2 cups Pepperidge Farm® Herb Seasoned Stuffing**
- **1 package (8 ounces) shredded mozzarella cheese (2 cups)**

1. Cook the beef in a 12-inch skillet over medium-high heat until the beef is well browned, stirring frequently to break up meat. Pour off any fat. Stir the soup, water and seasoning into the skillet.
2. Spoon the beef mixture into a 13×9×2-inch (3-quart) shallow baking dish. Add the stuffing and stir lightly to coat. Sprinkle with cheese.
3. Bake at 350°F. for 35 minutes or until golden brown and bubbly.

Makes: 6 servings

Cheesy Chicken Bake

PREP: 5 minutes • **BAKE:** 40 minutes

- **1 can (10¾ ounces) Campbell's® Condensed Cream of Chicken Soup (Regular or 98% Fat Free)**
- **1⅓ cups water**
- **1 teaspoon Worcestershire sauce**
- **¾ cup uncooked regular long-grain white rice**
- **2 cups cubed cooked chicken**
- **½ cup shredded Cheddar cheese**
- **1 can (2.8 ounces) French fried onions (1⅓ cups)**

1. Stir the soup, water, Worcestershire, rice, chicken and cheese in a 2-quart casserole. **Cover.**
2. Bake at 350°F. for 35 minutes or until hot. Stir.
3. Sprinkle with onions. Bake for 5 minutes more or until golden.

Makes: 4 servings

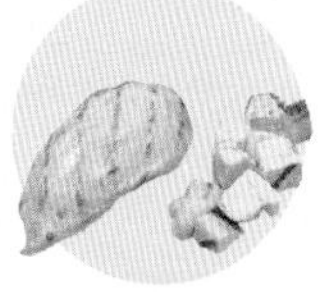

Cheese Strata

PREP: 15 minutes • **CHILL:** 4 hours
BAKE: 45 minutes • **STAND:** 10 minutes

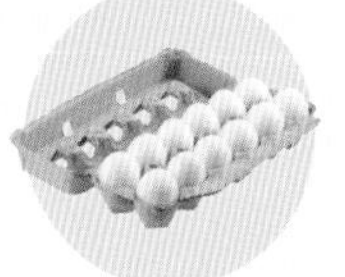

Vegetable cooking spray
6 slices Pepperidge Farm® Toasting White Bread, cut into cubes
1 can (10¾ ounces) Campbell's® Condensed Cheddar Cheese Soup
1 cup milk
4 eggs
1½ cups shredded Swiss cheese (6 ounces)

1. Spray an 11×8-inch (2-quart) shallow baking dish with cooking spray. Place the bread cubes in the prepared dish.
2. Stir the soup, milk and eggs in a small bowl with a whisk or a fork until the ingredients are mixed. Stir in the cheese. Pour over the bread. Cover the dish and refrigerate it for 4 hours or overnight. **Uncover**.
3. Bake at 350°F. for 45 minutes or until a knife inserted near the center comes out clean. Let the strata stand for 10 minutes before serving.

Makes: 6 servings

Cooking for a Crowd: *Recipe may be doubled. Double all ingredients. Divide evenly between 2 (11×8-inch) shallow baking dishes. Serves 12.*

Easy Substitution: *Use whole-grain bread and shredded Cheddar cheese for the white bread and Swiss cheese.*

Lemon Herb Chicken and Broccoli

PREP: 10 minutes • **BAKE:** 45 minutes

- **1 can (10¾ ounces) Campbell's® Condensed Cream of Chicken with Herbs Soup**
- **¾ cup water**
- **1 tablespoon lemon juice**
- **1 bag (16 ounces) frozen broccoli cuts, thawed (about 4 cups)**
- **1½ pounds skinless, boneless chicken breasts cut into 1-inch cubes**
- **½ cup dry bread crumbs**
- **2 tablespoons butter, melted**

1. Stir the soup, water, lemon juice, broccoli and chicken in a 13×9×2-inch (3-quart) shallow baking dish. **Cover.**

2. Bake at 375°F. for 40 minutes or until the chicken is cooked through. Stir.

3. Mix the bread crumbs with the butter in a small bowl and sprinkle over the chicken mixture. Bake for 5 minutes more or until golden brown.

Makes: 6 servings

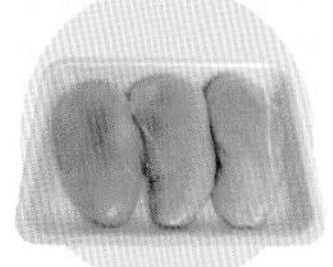

Time-Saving Tip: *To thaw the broccoli, cut off 1 corner of bag, microwave on HIGH for 3 minutes.*

Baked Chicken & Broccoli

PREP: 15 minutes • **BAKE:** 30 minutes

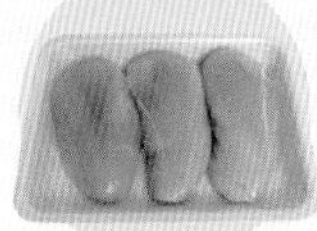

1 pound broccoli, trimmed, cut into 1-inch pieces, cooked and drained

8 skinless, boneless chicken breast halves

1 can (26 ounces) Campbell's® Condensed Cream of Mushroom Soup (Regular or 98% Fat Free)

⅔ cup milk

¼ teaspoon ground black pepper

Hot cooked rice

1. Place the broccoli and chicken in a 13×9×2-inch (3-quart) shallow baking dish. Stir the soup, milk and black pepper in a small bowl. Pour the soup mixture over the broccoli and chicken.

2. Bake at 400°F. for 30 minutes or until the chicken is cooked through. Stir the sauce before serving. Serve with rice.

Makes: 8 servings

Beefy Pasta Casserole

PREP: 15 minutes
BAKE: 30 minutes • **STAND:** 5 minutes

- 1 pound ground beef
- 1 tablespoon dried oregano leaves, crushed
- 2 cans (10¾ ounces **each**) Campbell's® Condensed Tomato Soup (Regular **or** Healthy Request®)
- 1 soup can water
- ½ of a 16-ounce package (4 cups) **uncooked** corkscrew-shaped pasta (rotini)
- 1 container (15 ounces) ricotta cheese
- 1 cup shredded mozzarella cheese (4 ounces)

1. Cook the beef and oregano in a 12-inch skillet over medium-high heat until the beef is well browned, stirring frequently to break up meat. Pour off any fat.

2. Stir the soup, water and pasta in a 13×9×2-inch (3-quart) shallow baking dish. Add the beef mixture and ricotta cheese and stir to coat. **Cover**.

3. Bake at 375°F. for 30 minutes or until hot and bubbly. Sprinkle with the mozzarella cheese. Let stand for 5 minutes or until the cheese melts.

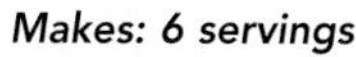

Makes: 6 servings

Tomato-Topped Chicken & Stuffing

PREP: 10 minutes • **BAKE:** 30 minutes

- **5 cups Pepperidge Farm® Cubed Herb Seasoned Stuffing**
- **6 tablespoons butter, melted**
- **1¼ cups boiling water**
- **4 skinless, boneless chicken breast halves**
- **1 can (10¾ ounces) Campbell's® Condensed Cream of Chicken Soup (Regular or 98% Fat Free)**
- **⅓ cup milk**
- **1 medium tomato, sliced**

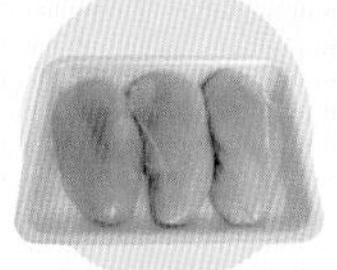

1. Coarsely crush **1 cup** of the stuffing. Mix crushed stuffing with **2 tablespoons** of the butter in a small bowl. Set aside.
2. Mix the remaining butter and water in a medium bowl. Add the stuffing and stir lightly to coat.
3. Spoon into a 13×9×2-inch (3-quart) shallow baking dish. Top with the chicken.
4. Stir the soup and milk in a small bowl. Pour over the chicken. Top with the tomato. Sprinkle with the reserved stuffing mixture.
5. Bake at 400°F. for 30 minutes or until chicken is cooked through.

Makes: 4 servings

Home-Style Chicken & Biscuits

PREP: 5 minutes • **BAKE:** 30 minutes

- **1 can (10¾ ounces) Campbell's® Condensed Cream of Chicken Soup (Regular or 98% Fat Free)**
- **¼ cup milk**

- **¼ teaspoon ground black pepper**
- **¾ cup shredded Cheddar cheese**

- **1 bag (16 ounces) frozen vegetable combination (broccoli, cauliflower, carrots)**

- **3 cups cubed cooked chicken**

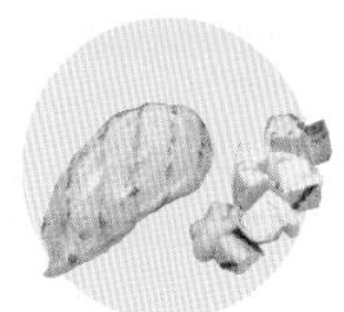

- **1 package (7.5 ounces) refrigerated biscuits (10)**

1. Stir the soup, milk, black pepper and cheese in a 13×9×2-inch (3-quart) shallow baking dish. Stir in the vegetables and chicken.
2. Bake at 400°F. for 15 minutes. Stir.
3. Top with the biscuits. Bake for 15 minutes more or until the biscuits are golden.

Makes: 6 servings

Creamy Chicken Florentine

PREP: 5 minutes
BAKE: 30 minutes • **STAND:** 5 minutes

- **1 can (10¾ ounces) Campbell's® Condensed Cream of Mushroom with Roasted Garlic Soup**
- **½ cup water**
- **1 package (10 ounces) frozen cut leaf spinach**
- **1 can (14.5 ounces) diced tomatoes with basil and oregano**
- **1½ pounds skinless, boneless chicken breasts cut into 1-inch cubes**
- **½ of 16-ounce package (about 3 cups) uncooked tube-shaped pasta (penne)**
- **½ cup shredded mozzarella cheese**

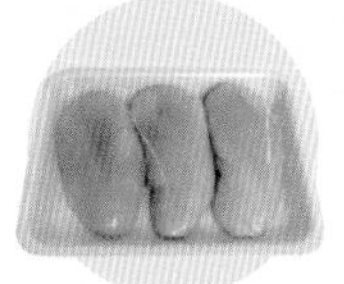

1. Stir the soup, water, spinach, tomatoes and chicken in a 13×9×2-inch (3-quart) shallow baking dish. **Cover**.
2. Bake at 375°F. for 20 minutes. Stir. While the chicken is baking, cook the pasta according to the package directions. Drain and stir the hot cooked pasta into the dish.
3. Bake for 10 minutes more or until hot and bubbly. Sprinkle with cheese. Let stand for 5 minutes or until the cheese melts.

Makes: 4 servings

Creamy Beef, Carrot and Noodle Baked Stroganoff

PREP: 10 minutes • **BAKE:** 30 minutes

1 pound ground beef

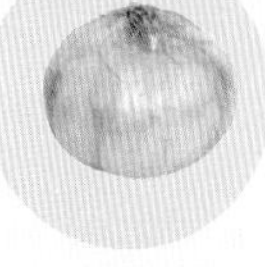

1 large onion, diced (about 1 cup)

2 cans (10¾ ounces **each**) Campbell's® Condensed Cream of Mushroom Soup (Regular **or** 98% Fat Free)

2 cups water

2 cups frozen crinkle-cut carrots, thawed

2 cups **uncooked** medium egg noodles

½ cup sour cream

1. Cook the beef and onion in a 12-inch skillet until the beef is well browned, stirring frequently to break up meat. Pour off any fat. Spoon the beef mixture into a 13×9×2-inch (3-quart) shallow baking dish. Stir the soup, water, carrots, noodles and sour cream into the dish. **Cover**.

2. Bake at 375°F. for 30 minutes or until hot and bubbly.

Makes: 6 servings

Cheesy Chile Corn Casserole

PREP: 10 minutes • **BAKE:** 30 minutes

1 can (10¾ ounces) Campbell's® Condensed Cheddar Cheese Soup
¼ cup milk
1 tablespoon butter, melted
Dash ground red pepper
1 bag (16 ounces) frozen whole kernel corn, thawed (about 3 cups)
1 can (4 ounces) diced green chilies
1 can (2.8 ounces) French fried onions (1⅓ cups)

1. Stir the soup, milk, butter, pepper, corn, chilies and **⅔ cup** of the onions in a 1½-quart casserole.

2. Bake at 350°F. for 25 minutes. Stir the vegetable mixture.

3. Sprinkle the remaining onions over the vegetable mixture. Bake for 5 minutes more or until the onions are golden brown.

***Makes:** 6 servings*

Time-Saving Tip: *To thaw the corn, cut off 1 corner of bag, microwave on HIGH for 3 minutes.*

Chicken & Roasted Garlic Risotto

PREP: 5 minutes
BAKE: 40 minutes • **STAND:** 5 minutes

- 1 can (10¾ ounces) Campbell's® Condensed Cream of Chicken Soup (Regular **or** 98% Fat Free)
- 1 can (10¾ ounces) Campbell's® Condensed Cream of Mushroom with Roasted Garlic Soup
- 2 cups water
- 1 package (10 ounces) frozen peas and carrots (about 2 cups)
- 1 cup **uncooked** regular long-grain white rice
- 6 skinless, boneless chicken breast halves
- ¼ cup grated Parmesan cheese

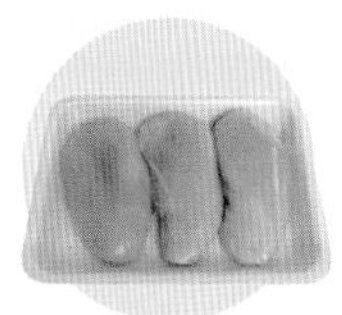

1. Stir the soups, water, vegetables and rice in a 13×9×2-inch (3-quart) shallow baking dish. Top with the chicken. **Cover**.

2. Bake at 375°F. for 40 minutes or until the chicken is cooked through. Sprinkle with cheese. Let stand for 5 minutes.

Makes: 6 servings

Cauliflower Gratin

PREP: 10 minutes • **BAKE:** 50 minutes

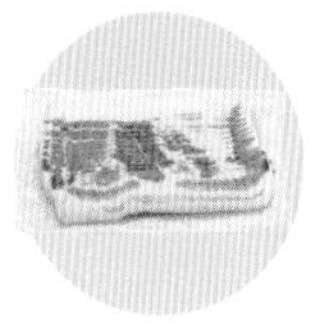

Vegetable cooking spray
1 can (10¾ ounces) Campbell's® Condensed Cream of Mushroom Soup (Regular or 98% Fat Free)
½ cup milk
1 clove garlic, minced
1 bag (20 ounces) frozen cauliflower flowerets, thawed (about 5 cups)
1 cup finely grated Swiss cheese (4 ounces)
¼ cup cooked crumbled bacon or real bacon bits

1. Spray an 11×8-inch (2-quart) shallow baking dish with cooking spray. Stir the soup, milk, garlic, cauliflower, and **½ cup** of the cheese in the casserole. Sprinkle with the bacon and remaining cheese.

2. Bake at 350°F. for 50 minutes or until the cauliflower is tender and mixture is hot and bubbly.

Makes: 6 servings

Cheddar Broccoli Bake

PREP: 10 minutes • **BAKE:** 30 minutes

1 can (10¾ ounces) Campbell's® Condensed Cheddar Cheese Soup
½ cup milk
Dash ground black pepper
4 cups cooked broccoli cuts
1 can (2.8 ounces) French fried onions (1⅓ cups)

1. Stir the soup, milk, black pepper, broccoli and **⅔ cup** of the onions in a 1½-quart casserole. **Cover**.

2. Bake at 350°F. for 25 minutes or until hot. Stir the broccoli mixture.

3. Sprinkle the remaining onions over the broccoli mixture. Bake for 5 minutes more or until the onions are golden.

Makes: 6 servings

Easy Substitution Tip: *Omit the onions. In step 3, sprinkle* ***¼ cup*** *dry breadcrumbs over the broccoli mixture.*

Creamy Souper Rice

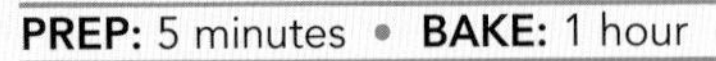

PREP: 5 minutes • **BAKE:** 1 hour

- **1 can (10¾ ounces) Campbell's® Condensed Cream of Mushroom Soup (Regular or 98% Fat Free)**
- **1⅓ cups water**
- **¾ cup uncooked regular long-grain white rice**

1. Stir the soup, water and rice in a 1-quart casserole. **Cover**.
2. Bake at 375°F. for 30 minutes. Stir.
3. Bake for 30 minutes more or until the rice is tender. Stir the rice before serving.

Makes: 4 servings

Green Bean Casserole

PREP: 10 minutes • **BAKE:** 30 minutes

- **1 can (10¾ ounces) Campbell's® Condensed Cream of Mushroom Soup (Regular or 98% Fat Free)**
- **½ cup milk**
- **1 teaspoon soy sauce**
- **Dash ground black pepper**
- **2 packages (10 ounces each) frozen cut green beans, cooked and drained**
- **1 can (2.8 ounces) French fried onions (1⅓ cups)**

1. Stir the soup, milk, soy sauce, black pepper, green beans and **⅔ cup** of the onions in a 1½-quart casserole.

2. Bake at 350°F. for 25 minutes or until hot. Stir the green bean mixture.

3. Sprinkle the remaining onions over the green bean mixture. Bake for 5 minutes more or until the onions are golden brown.

Makes: 6 servings

Campbell's Kitchen Tip: *You can also make this classic side dish with fresh or canned green beans. You will need either 1½ pounds fresh green beans, cut into 1-inch pieces, cooked and drained* ***or*** *2 cans (about 16 ounces* ***each****) cut green beans, drained for the frozen green beans.*

Creamy 3-Cheese Pasta

PREP: 20 minutes • **BAKE:** 20 minutes

- 1 can (10¾ ounces) Campbell's® Condensed Cream of Mushroom Soup (Regular **or** 98% Fat Free)
- 1 cup milk
- ¼ teaspoon ground black pepper
- 1 package (8 ounces) shredded two-cheese blend
- ⅓ cup grated Parmesan cheese
- 3 cups corkscrew-shaped pasta (rotini), cooked and drained

1. Stir the soup, milk, black pepper and cheeses in a 1½-quart casserole. Stir in the pasta.
2. Bake at 400°F. for 20 minutes or until hot.
3. Stir before serving.

Makes: 4 servings

Creamy Baked Carrots

PREP: 5 minutes • **BAKE:** 40 minutes

- **Vegetable cooking spray**
- **1 can (10¾ ounces) Campbell's® Condensed Cream of Celery Soup (Regular or 98% Fat Free)**
- **½ cup milk**
- **½ teaspoon dried thyme leaves, crushed**
- **1 bag (20 ounces) frozen crinkle-cut carrots, thawed (about 5 cups)**
- **1 can (2.8 ounces) French fried onions (1⅓ cups)**

1. Spray a 2-quart casserole with cooking spray. Stir the soup, milk, thyme, carrots, and **⅔ cup** of the onions in the prepared dish.
2. Bake at 350°F. for 35 minutes. Stir the carrot mixture.

3. Sprinkle the remaining onions over the carrot mixture. Bake for 5 minutes more or until carrots are tender and onions are golden brown.

Makes: 6 servings

Golden Onions & Spinach Bake

PREP: 5 minutes • **BAKE:** 25 minutes

1 can (10¾ ounces) Campbell's® Condensed Cream of Celery Soup (Regular or 98% Fat Free)
¼ cup sour cream
2 tablespoons grated Parmesan cheese
¼ teaspoon ground nutmeg
2 packages (about 10 ounces each) frozen chopped spinach, thawed and drained
1 can (2.8 ounces) French fried onions (1⅓ cups)

1. Stir the soup, sour cream, cheese, nutmeg, spinach and **⅔ cup** of the onions in a 1½-quart casserole. **Cover**.

2. Bake at 350°F. for 20 minutes. Stir the spinach mixture.

3. Sprinkle the remaining onions over the spinach mixture. Bake for 5 minutes more or until the onions are golden brown.

***Makes:** 6 servings*

***Time-Saving Tip:** To thaw the spinach, microwave on HIGH for 3 minutes, breaking apart with a fork halfway through heating.*

Creamy Corn and Vegetable Orzo Casserole

PREP: 10 minutes • **BAKE:** 25 minutes

1 can (10¾ ounces) Campbell's® Condensed Cream of Celery Soup (Regular or 98% Fat Free)

1 cup water

1 bag (16 ounces) frozen whole kernel corn (2½ cups)

1 package (10 ounces) frozen vegetables (peas and carrots or cut green beans) (about 2 cups)

4 medium green onions, sliced (about ½ cup)

½ of a 16-ounce package (1½ cups) rice-shaped pasta (orzo), cooked and drained

1. Stir the soup, water, corn, vegetables, green onions and pasta into an 11×8-inch (2-quart) shallow baking dish. **Cover.**

2. Bake at 350°F. for 25 minutes or until hot and bubbly. Serve immediately.

Makes: 6 servings

Swiss Medley Casserole

PREP: 5 minutes • **BAKE:** 45 minutes

- 1 can (10¾ ounces) Campbell's® Condensed Cream of Chicken Soup (Regular **or** 98% Fat Free)
- ⅓ cup sour cream
- ¼ teaspoon ground black pepper
- 1 bag (16 ounces) frozen vegetable combination (broccoli, cauliflower, carrots), thawed
- 1 can (2.8 ounces) French fried onions (1⅓ cups)
- 1 cup shredded Swiss cheese (4 ounces)

1. Stir the soup, sour cream, black pepper, vegetables, **⅔ cup** of the onions and **½ cup** of the cheese in a 2-quart casserole. **Cover**.

2. Bake at 350°F. for 40 minutes or until the vegetables are tender. Stir.

3. Sprinkle with the remaining cheese and onions. Bake for 5 minutes more or until onions are golden.

Makes: 4 servings

Scalloped Potato-Onion Bake

PREP: 10 minutes • **BAKE:** 1 hour 15 minutes

- **1 can (10¾ ounces) Campbell's® Condensed Cream of Celery Soup (Regular or 98% Fat Free)**
- **½ cup milk**
- **Dash ground black pepper**
- **4 medium potatoes (about 1¼ pounds), thinly sliced**
- **1 small onion, thinly sliced (about ¼ cup)**
- **1 tablespoon butter, cut into pieces**
- **Paprika**

1. Stir the soup, milk and black pepper with a whisk or fork in a small bowl. Layer **half** of the potatoes, **half** of the onion and **half** of the soup mixture in a 1½-quart casserole. Repeat the layers. Place the butter over the soup mixture. Sprinkle with the paprika. **Cover**.

2. Bake at 400°F. for 1 hour. Uncover and bake for 15 minutes more or until the potatoes are fork-tender.

Makes: 6 servings

Saucy Asparagus Casserole

PREP: 5 minutes • **BAKE:** 20 minutes

2 pounds asparagus, trimmed

1 can (10¾ ounces) Campbell's® Condensed Cream of Asparagus Soup

⅓ cup milk or water

½ cup dry bread crumbs

2 tablespoons butter, melted

1. Place the asparagus in a 13×9×2-inch (3-quart) shallow baking dish.

2. Stir the soup and milk in a small bowl and pour over the asparagus. Mix the bread crumbs with the butter in a small bowl and sprinkle over the soup mixture.

3. Bake at 400°F. for 20 minutes or until golden brown and bubbly.

Makes: 6 servings

Easy Substitution: *Use 2 packages (about 10 ounces **each**) frozen asparagus spears, thawed, for the fresh asparagus.*

Roasted Potatoes with Thyme

PREP: 10 minutes • **BAKE:** 50 minutes

4 medium potatoes (about 1¼ pounds), sliced ¼ inch thick

1 teaspoon dried thyme leaves, crushed

¼ teaspoon ground black pepper

3 tablespoons vegetable oil

1 can (10¾ ounces) Campbell's® Condensed Golden Mushroom Soup

½ cup water

1 can (2.8 ounces) French fried onions (1⅓ cups)

1. Stir the potatoes, thyme, black pepper and oil in a 13×9×2-inch (3-quart) shallow baking dish in a single layer.

2. Bake at 400°F. for 20 minutes. Stir. Bake for 15 minutes more or until the potatoes are fork-tender and golden brown.

3. Reduce the temperature to 350°F. Stir the soup and water in a small bowl. Pour soup mixture over the potatoes. Sprinkle with the onions. Bake for 15 minutes more or until hot and bubbly. Serve immediately.

Makes: 4 servings

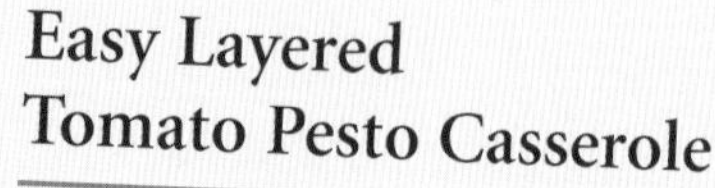

Easy Layered Tomato Pesto Casserole

PREP: 10 minutes
BAKE: 40 minutes • **STAND:** 5 minutes

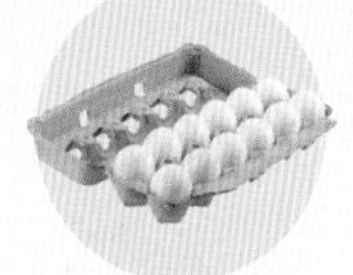

Vegetable cooking spray
2 cans (10¾ ounces each) Campbell's® Condensed Tomato Soup (Regular or Healthy Request®)
1½ cups milk
3 eggs
1 container (7 ounces) prepared pesto sauce
8 slices Pepperidge Farm® Hearty White Farmhouse™ Bread
1 package (8 ounces) shredded Italian cheese blend

1. Spray a 13×9×2-inch (3-quart) shallow baking dish with cooking spray. Stir the soup, milk and eggs in a 1-quart measuring cup or bowl until the ingredients are mixed. Spoon **½ cup** of the soup mixture into the prepared dish.

2. Spread about **1 tablespoon** of the pesto sauce on each bread slice. Place **4** slices in dish. Top with **½ cup** of the cheese. Carefully pour about **half** of the soup mixture over bread and cheese. Repeat layers with remaining bread slices, **½ cup** cheese and remaining soup mixture, making sure bread is coated with the soup mixture.

3. Bake at 350°F. for 40 minutes or until center is set. Sprinkle with the remaining cheese. Let stand for 5 minutes or until the cheese melts.

***Makes:* 8 servin**